ESSENTIAL KEYBOARD DUETS

25 INTERMEDIATE/LATE INTERMEDIATE SELECTIONS
IN THEIR ORIGINAL FORM

Classical to Modern

Cover photo: © AKG photo "Making Music" by Wilhelm von Linden-Schmit

SELECTED AND EDITED BY
GAYLE KOWALCHYK AND E. L. LANCASTER

ISBN 0-7390-2320-9

ESSENTIAL KEYBOARD DUETS, Vol. 2

25 Intermediate/Late Intermediate Selections

in Their Original Form

Classical to Modern

Selected and Edited by Gayle Kowalchyk and E. L. Lancaster

Historical Background

The music written for piano duet (one piano, four hands) is extremely diverse. The piano duet is the only medium where two people perform music written or arranged for a single instrument. The repertoire includes literature for every level of technical proficiency, from beginner to concert artist. It includes music written for pedagogical purposes, music for social occasions (especially popular in the 19th century), concert pieces and transcriptions.

The first known works for keyboard duet were written by two English composers in the early-17th century: *A Verse to Play on One Virginal or Organ,* by Nicholas Carlton, and *A Fancy for Two to Play,* by Thomas Tomkins. The first published duets, *Four Sonatas or Duets for Two Performers on One Piano Forte or Harpsichord,* by Charles Burney, were released in London in 1777. Prior to that, in 1765, Wolfgang Amadeus Mozart and his sister Nannerl performed his four-hand *Sonata in C Major,* K. 19d, in London. Johann Christian Bach was the first composer to write several works for the medium.

About This Collection

This collection includes a variety of repertoire originally written for the piano duet medium, appropriate for pianists at the intermediate through late intermediate levels. Many of the duets contain *primo* and *secondo* parts of equal difficulty; other duets were written for teacher and student, or for two students at different levels. In most of the duets, both parts have melodic interest. However, a few with melodic material only in the *primo* part have been included for historical reasons. The pieces are arranged chronologically by the composer's birth date. In many ways, the selections provide a historical guide to the piano duet repertoire at these levels, for the 18th, 19th and early-20th centuries.

Features of This Edition

- Each duet has been carefully edited and fingered for performance ease.
- To facilitate reading, the *primo* and *secondo* parts are on separate pages.
- Essential ornamentation is realized in footnotes.
- Both parts contain measure numbers for convenient reference.
- Brief biographies of the composers represented in the collection are found on pages 158–160.

All specific pedal markings are by the composers. The editors have added the indication "with pedal" to the *secondo* part of other duets, if needed. Final decisions on using pedal depend on the piano, the acoustics of the room, the level of the performers, and musical considerations such as the tempo of the piece.

Balance between the two parts is crucial in duet playing. While some composers suggest a louder dynamic level for the more prominent part, others indicate the same level for both parts. Students will need to be aware of how dynamics in the two parts relate to each other in terms of melodic importance.

Pedagogical Value

Duets provide a social outlet for students who practice solo repertoire most of the time. Teachers recognize the importance of piano duets in developing musicianship, ensemble performance, sight reading skills and rhythmic control. These duets can be used as supplementary material for any method or course of study. In addition, they make excellent repertoire selections for group lessons, ensemble classes or "monster" concerts. Students will be motivated by music-making with friends, while developing skills in duet performance.

Contents Listed by Composer

ANDANTINO CON MOTO

from *Sonata in C Major*

SECONDO

Jan Ladislav Dussek (1760–1812)

Op. 67, No. 1

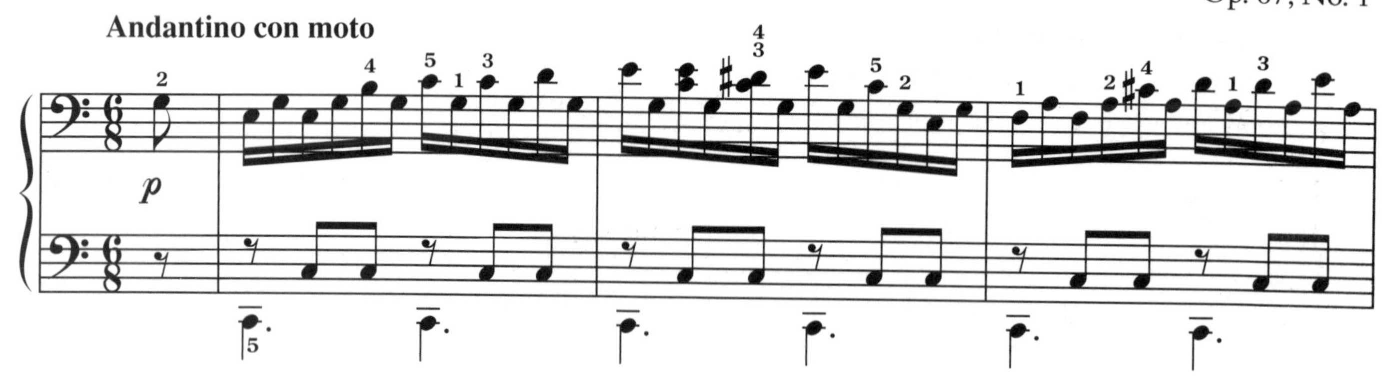

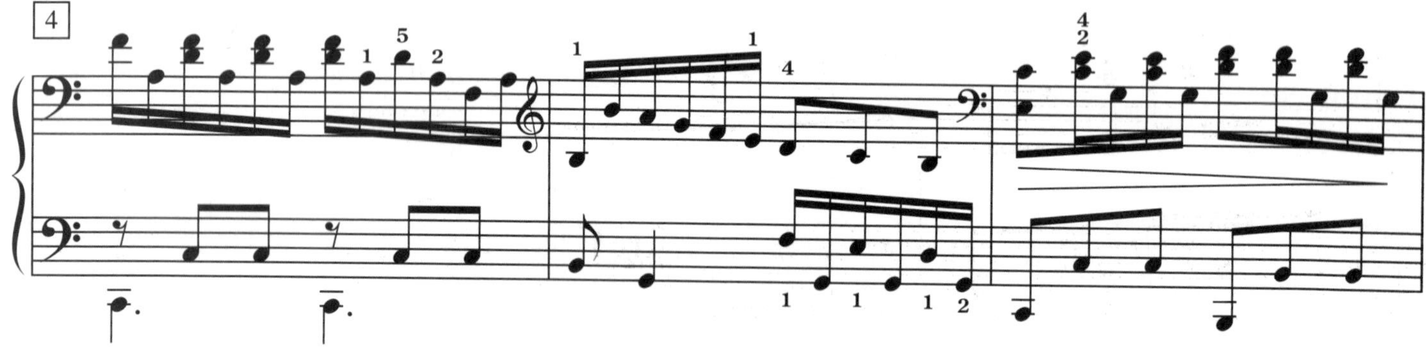

Andantino con moto

from *Sonata in C Major*

PRIMO

Jan Ladislav Dussek (1760–1812)

Op. 67, No. 1

Andantino con moto

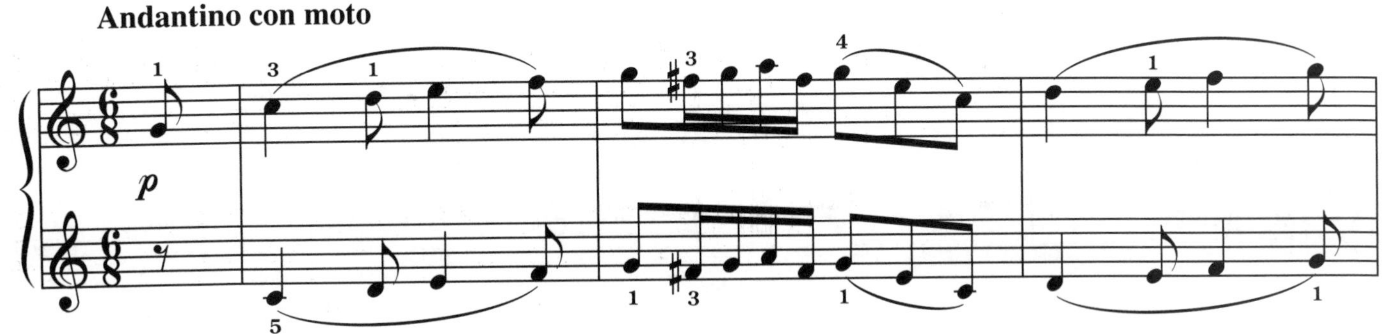

13
mf
16
rf
19
rf
22
f
26

13
mf
16
rf
19
rf
22
f
26

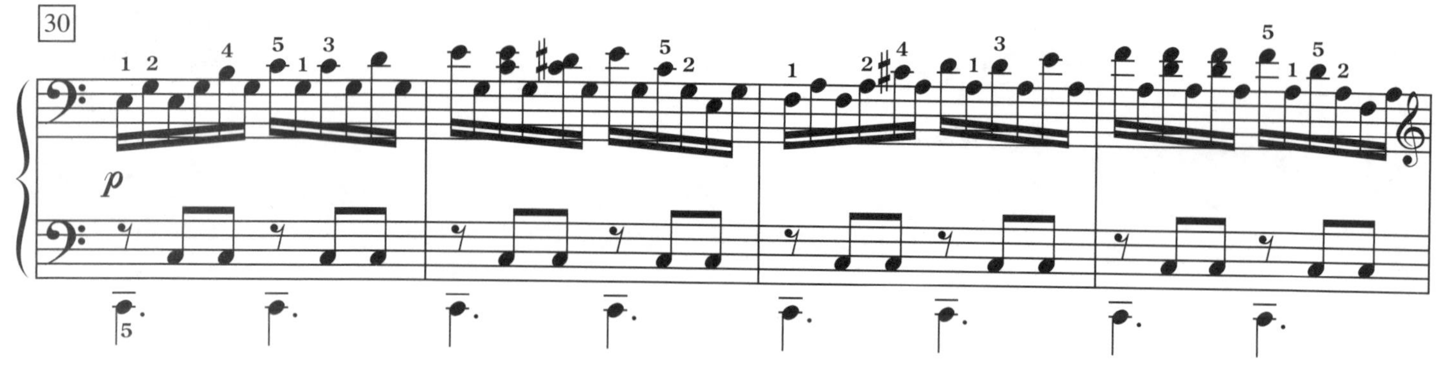
30
p

34
cresc.

37
f

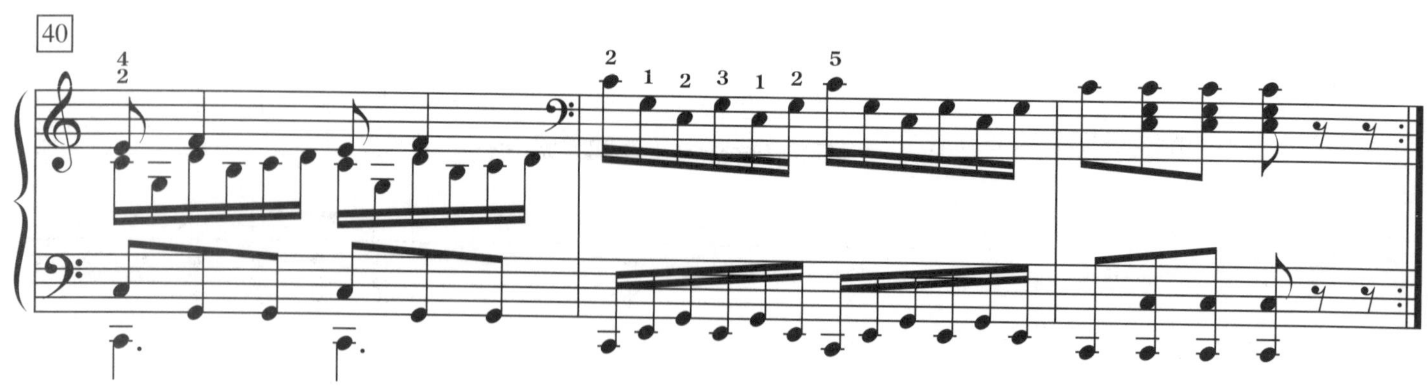
40

30
p

34
cresc.

37
f

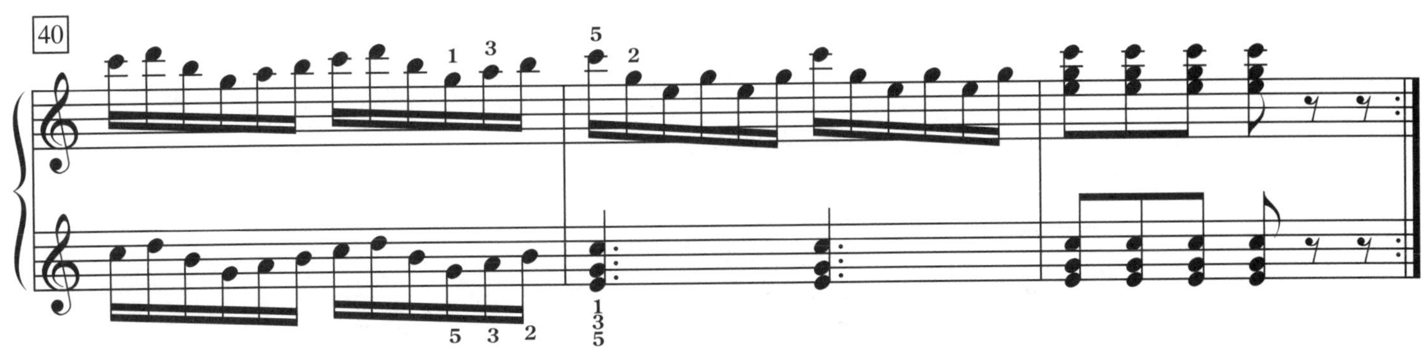
40

Allegro molto

from *Sonata in D Major*

SECONDO

Ludwig van Beethoven (1770–1827)

Op. 6

Allegro molto

from *Sonata in D Major*

PRIMO

Ludwig van Beethoven (1770–1827)

Op. 6

Allegro molto

f *p*

6

11

16

21

cresc. *ff*

ⓐ Play the grace notes slightly before the beat.

26
p
32
37
p
cresc.
f
sf
42
sf
sf
sf
47
52

SECONDO

57
ff
fp
63
ff
68
fp
73
p
78
pp
83
ff

SECONDO

ⓐ Play the grace notes slightly before the beat.

123
sf
sf
129
sf
p dolce
135
cresc.
f
sf
sf
140
sf
sf
146
ff
152
sf
ff

123
p
129
135
p cresc.
f
sf
sf
140
f
sf
sf
146
ff
152
sf
ff

Sonatina in D Major

SECONDO

Anton André (1775–1842)
Op. 45, No. 5

Sonatina in D Major

PRIMO

Anton André (1775–1842)
Op. 45, No. 5

Alla Polacca

Alla Polacca

Rondo

from *Pleasures of Youth*

SECONDO

Anton Diabelli (1781–1858)

Op. 163, No. 6

Rondo

from *Pleasures of Youth*

PRIMO

Anton Diabelli (1781–1858)
Op. 163, No. 6

25
p
30
f
p
35
39
f
p
44
f

25
(RH 8va throughout)
30
35
39
44

ⓐ Play the grace notes slightly before the beat.

ⓐ Play the grace notes slightly before the beat.

ALLEGRO

from *Sonatina in G Major*

SECONDO

Friedrich Kuhlau (1786–1832)

Op. 44, No. 1

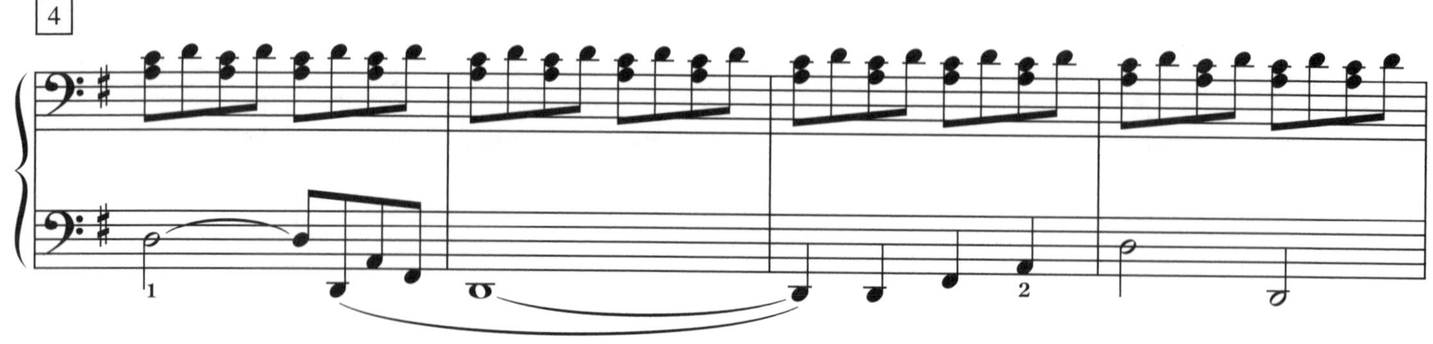

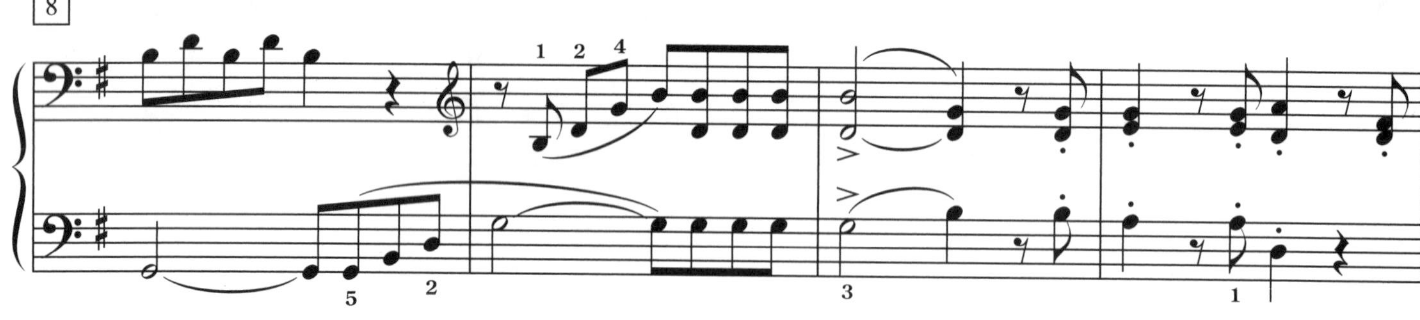

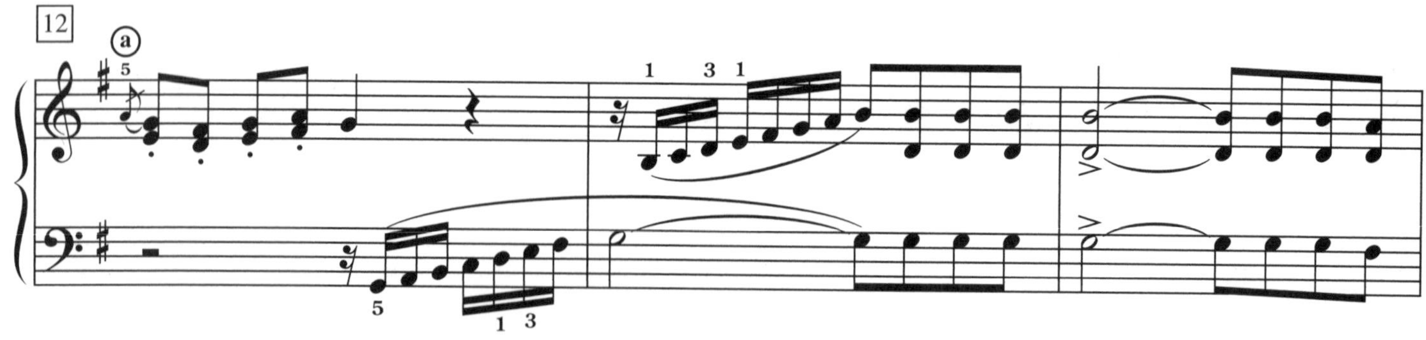

ⓐ Play the grace notes slightly before the beat.

Allegro

from *Sonatina in G Major*

PRIMO

Friedrich Kuhlau (1786–1832)

Op. 44, No. 1

18
f
p
21
24
27
30
mf
33
sf

18
8va
f
dim.
21
p
24
27
8va
30
a
mf
33
sf
a

36
dolce
39
42
cresc.
45
48
51
dim.

36
dolce
39
42
8va
cresc.
45
dim.
48
51
dim.

54
57
60
63
66
69
1.
2.
mf
sf
f

54
8va
p
57
60
63
66
mf
69
1.
2.
sf
f

Allegro moderato

from *Sonatina in C Major*

SECONDO

Carl Czerny (1791–1857)

Op. 156, No. 1

Allegro moderato

from *Sonatina in C Major*

PRIMO

Carl Czerny (1791–1857)

Op. 156, No. 1

ⓐ Play the grace notes slightly before the beat.

20
p
cresc.
23
f
26
p
dolce
30
cresc.
f
34
p

20
8va
p
cresc.
23
f
26
p dolce
30
cresc.
f
34
p dolce

38
41
44
47
50
f
p
cresc.
f
ff

38
(8va)
41
sf
f
44
p dolce
47
cresc.
f
50
ff

Waltz and Trio No. 5

SECONDO

Ignaz Moscheles
(1794–1870)

*Tempo marking is editorial.

Waltz and Trio No. 5

PRIMO

Ignaz Moscheles
(1794–1870)

*Tempo marking is editorial.

Trio

f *p* *ff* *sf* *sf* *pp*

Trio
f
p
5
9
dolce
13
ff
sf
sf
p
17

21
25
29
33
37
sf
ff
f
p

21
25
29
33
37
sf
f
p
cresc.

Two Ländler

SECONDO

Franz Schubert (1797–1828)

*Tempo marking is editorial.

Two Ländler

PRIMO

Franz Schubert (1797–1828)
D. 814, No. 1

*Tempo marking is editorial.

Gartenmelodie
SECONDO

Robert Schumann (1810–1856)
Op. 85, No. 3

GARTENMELODIE

PRIMO

Robert Schumann (1810–1856)
Op. 85, No. 3

ⓐ Play the grace notes slightly before the beat.

21
p
26
31
fp
36
p
41
46
fp

p
fp
p
fp

The Russians Are Coming

SECONDO

Robert Volkmann (1815–1883)

Op. 11, No. 3

The Russians Are Coming

PRIMO

Robert Volkmann (1815–1883)

Op. 11, No. 3

35
simile
42
cresc.
49
f
55
p
61
68

35
42
cresc.
49
f
55
8va
p
61
68

SECONDO

75

f

81

p

88

ff

95

p

102

cresc.

f

109

PRIMO

March in C Major

SECONDO

Niels Wilhelm Gade (1817–1890)
Op. 18, No. 1

March in C Major

PRIMO

Niels Wilhelm Gade (1817–1890)

Op. 18, No. 1

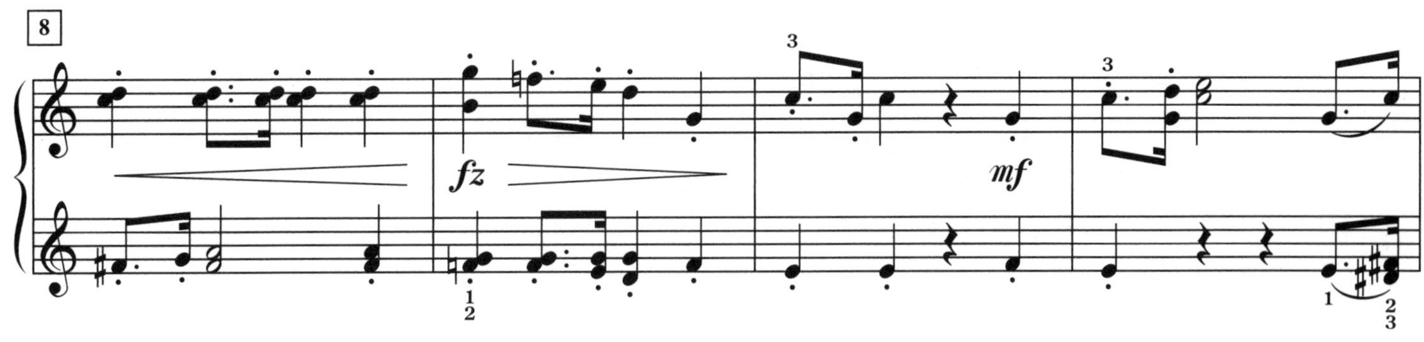

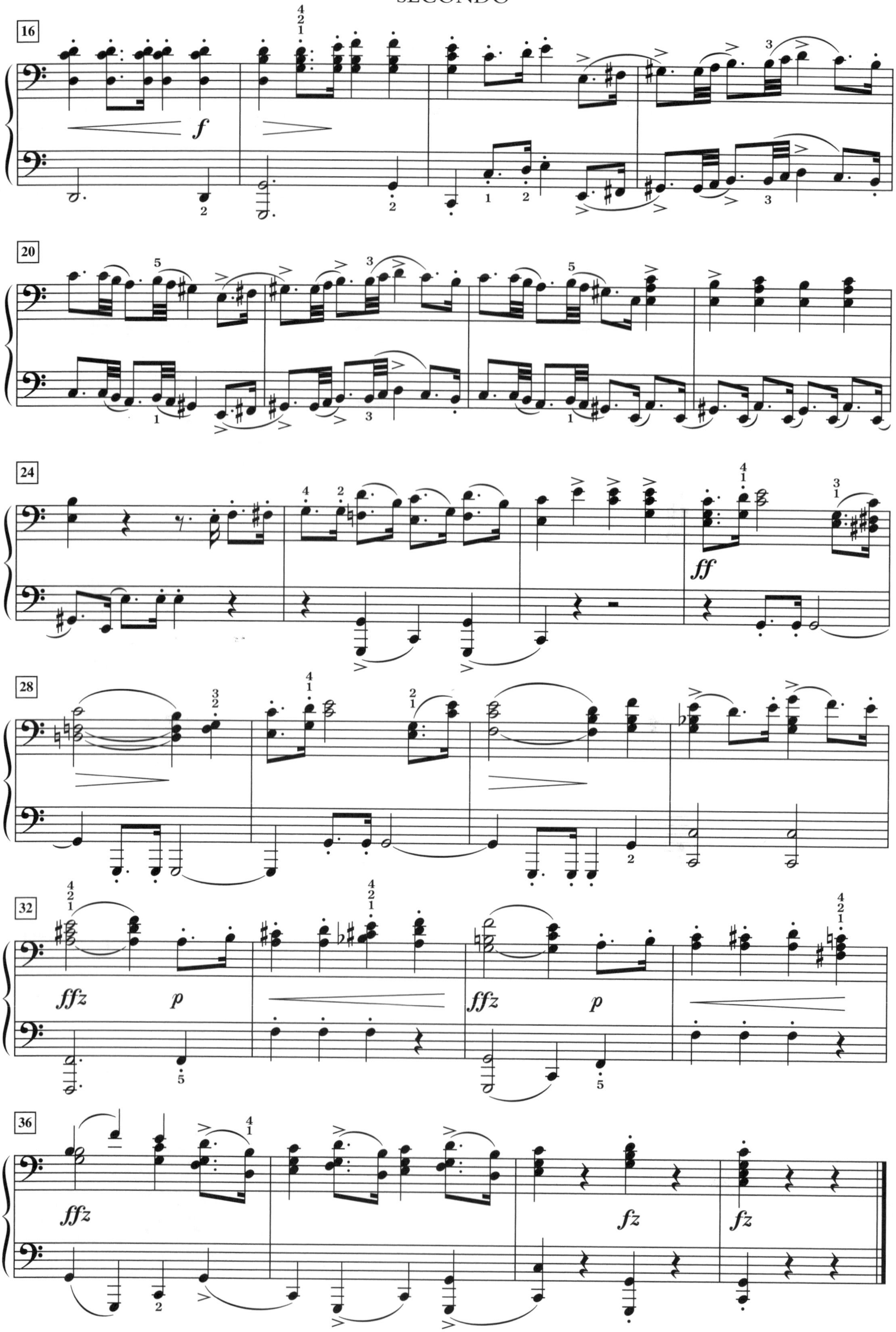
16
f
20
24
ff
28
32
ffz
p
ffz
p
36
ffz
fz
fz

16
f
20
8va
24
ff
28
32
ffz
p
ffz
p
36
ffz
fz
fz

Allegro moderato

from *Sonata Miniature*

SECONDO

Carl Reinecke
(1824–1910)

ⓐ Play the grace notes slightly before the beat.

Allegro moderato

from *Sonata Miniature*

PRIMO

Carl Reinecke
(1824–1910)

ⓐ Play the grace notes slightly before the beat.

26
pp
1.
32
2.
mf
f
37
42
fp
47
cresc.
f
52
mf
dim.
p

26
1.
pp
32
2.
mf
8va
f
37
42
sf
sf
fp
47
cresc.
f
dim.
52
mf
p

58
pp
64
p
mf
70
cresc.
f
75
mf
80
pp
86
pp

58
pp
p
64
mf
70
cresc.
f
75
mf
80
8va
pp
86
pp

Waltz in A Major

SECONDO

Johannes Brahms (1833–1897)

Op. 39, No. 15

*Tempo marking is editorial.

Waltz in A Major

PRIMO

Johannes Brahms (1833–1897)

Op. 39, No. 15

*Tempo marking is editorial.

ⓐ Play the grace notes slightly before the beat.

Le bal

from *Jeux d'enfants*

SECONDO

Georges Bizet (1838–1875)
Op. 22, No. 12

Le bal

from *Jeux d'enfants*

PRIMO

Georges Bizet (1838–1875)
Op. 22, No. 12

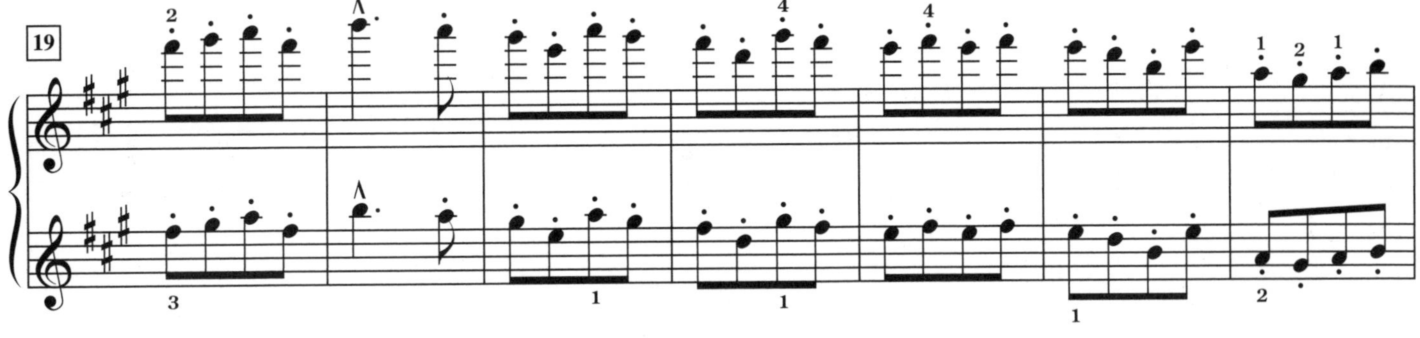

ⓐ Play the grace notes slightly before the beat.

33
p
f
p
39
f
pp
cresc.
ff
45
tutta forza
50
55
ppp
60

33
f
p
39
f
pp
cresc.
ff
45
tutta forza
50
55
60
ppp
8va
aussi pp que possible

65
aussi pp que possible
70
75
ten.
ten.
79
ten.
ten.
83
poco a poco cresc. molto
87

65 (8va)

ten.

70

75

79

83 poco a poco cresc. molto

87

92
ff
98
104
p
110
f
p
116
f
pp
cresc.
ff
122
tutta forza

Double an octave lower for LH; starting finger 2.

128
pp
134
cresc. molto
139
fff furioso
145
151
157

128
pp
134
cresc. molto
139
fff furioso
145
151
157

GALOP

from *Precipitevolissimevolmente*

SECONDO

Ernesto Becucci (1845–1905)

Op. 266, No. 1

Galop

from *Precipitevolissimevolmente*

PRIMO

Ernesto Becucci (1845–1905)

Op. 266, No. 1

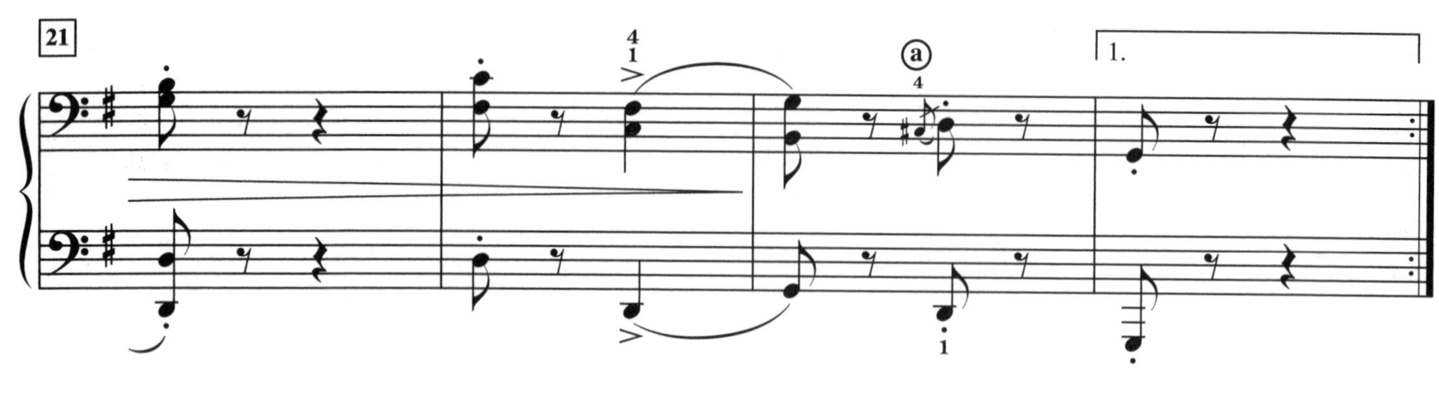

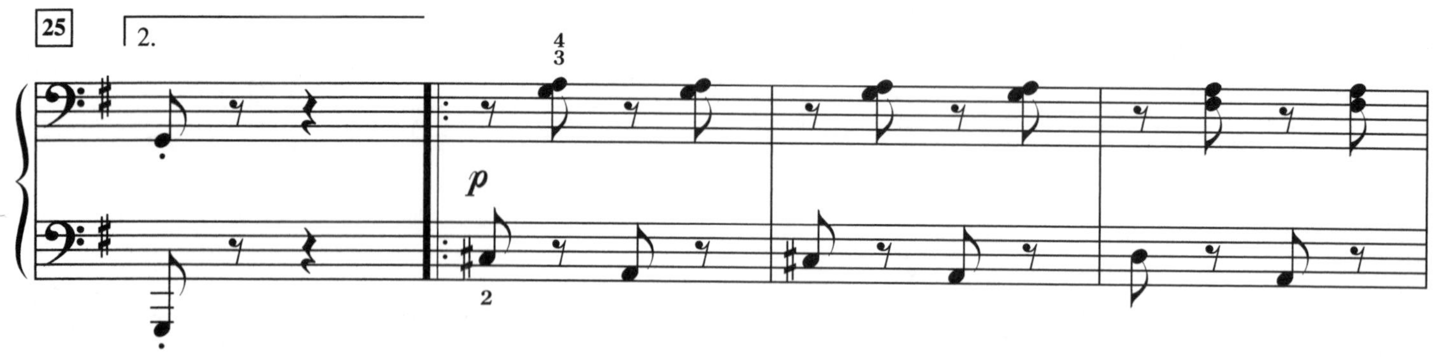

ⓐ Play the grace note on the beat, almost together with the note that follows.

(8va)
21
1.
p
25
2.
p
29
8va
33
p
37
8va
1.
f
p

42
2.
p
47
51
cresc.
55
59
p
63
sf

42
2.
(8va)
p
47
51
cresc.
8va
55
p
59
63

67
p
71
cresc.
f
1.
75
2.
ff
79
pp
83
ff
87
p
1.

67
p
71
cresc.
f
1.
p
75
2.
8va
ff
79
pp
83
ff
87
p
1.
ff

92
2.
p
97
101
cresc.
105
string.
109

92
2.
p
97
101
cresc.
8va
105
string.
109
8va

Berceuse

from *Dolly*

SECONDO

Gabriel Fauré (1845–1924)

Op. 56, No. 1

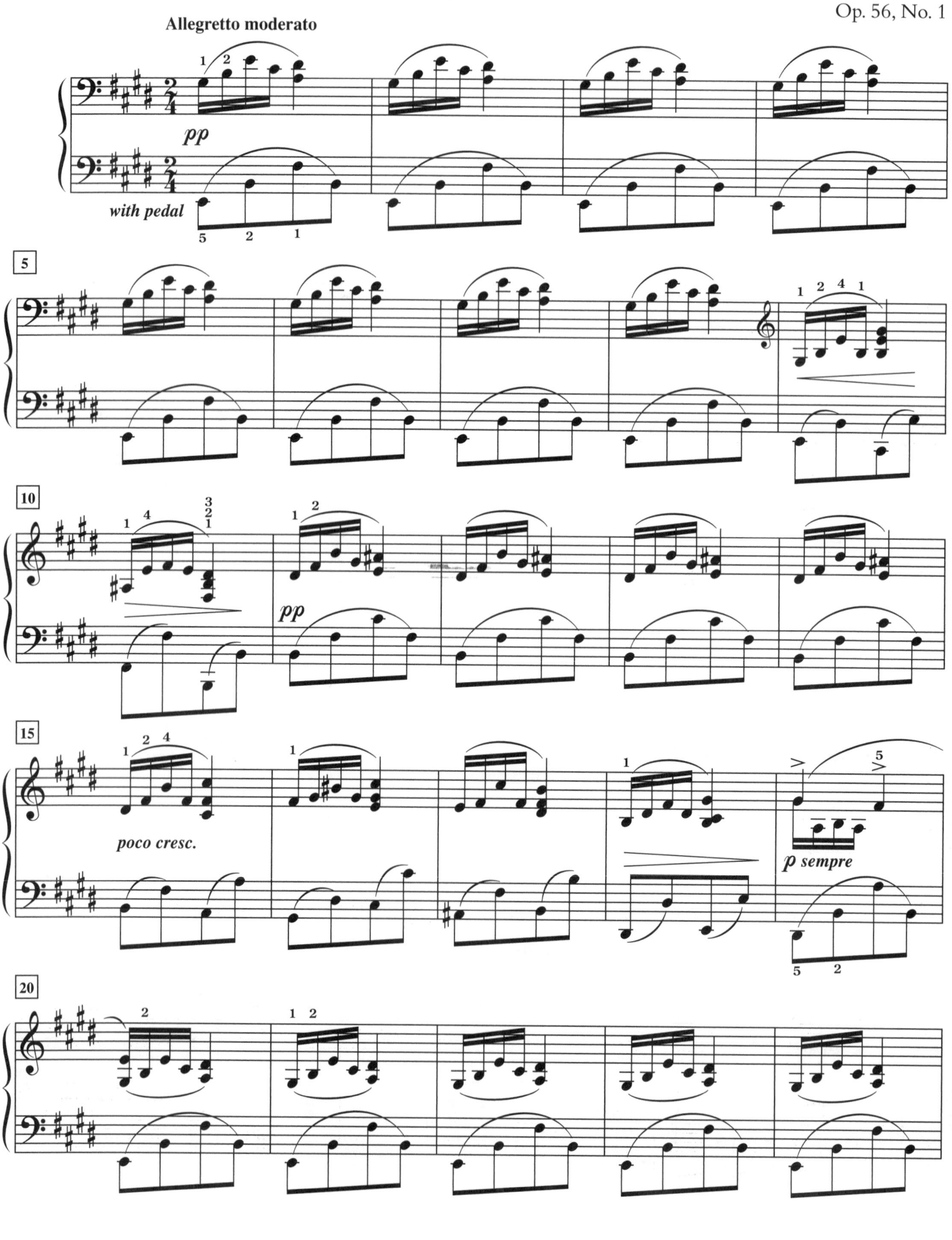

Allegretto moderato

pp

with pedal

pp

poco cresc.

p sempre

BERCEUSE

from *Dolly*

PRIMO

Gabriel Fauré (1845–1924)

Op. 56, No. 1

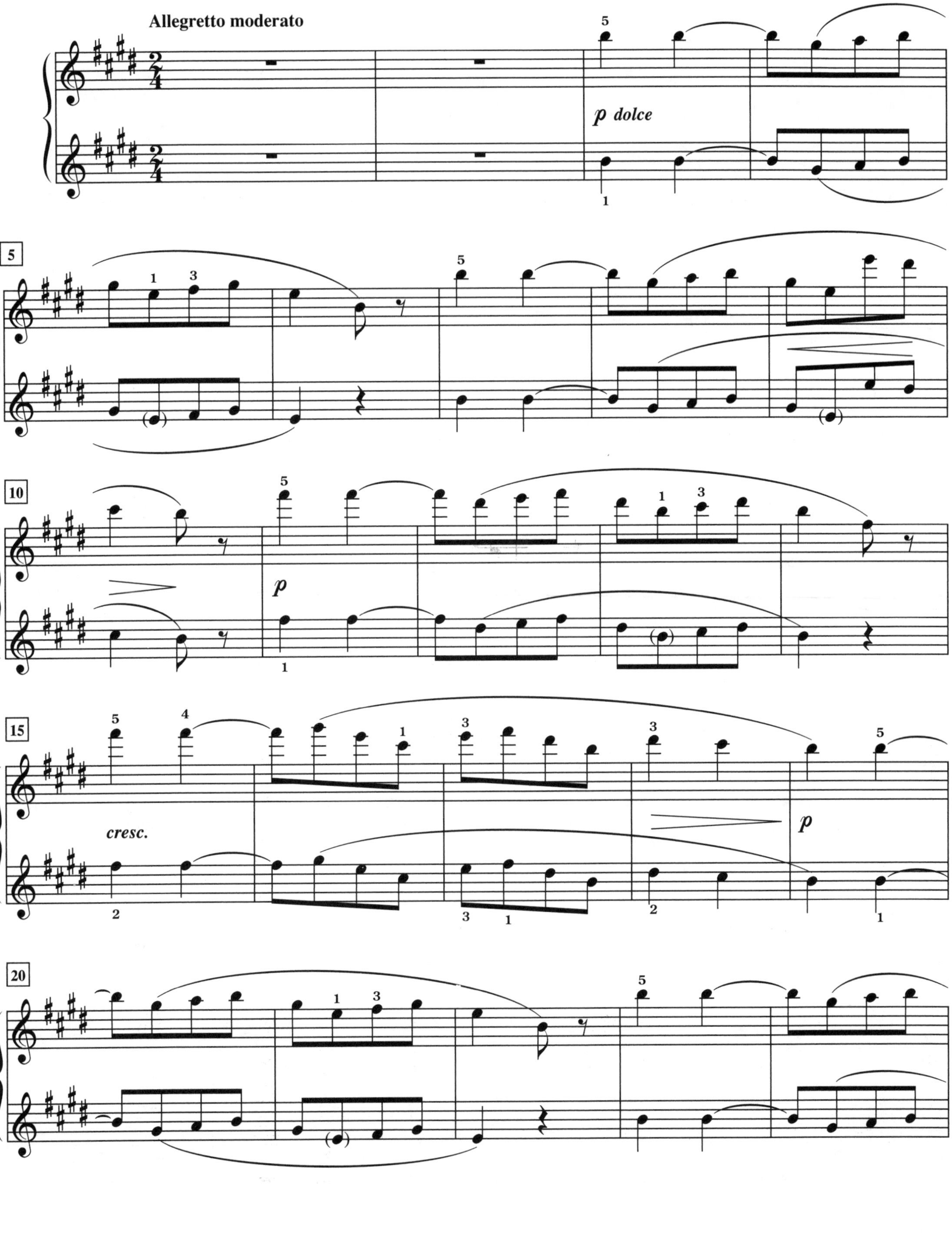

Allegretto moderato

p dolce

p

cresc.

p

SECONDO

25
cresc.
30
8va
f
p
35
sempre dolce
40
45
50
cresc.

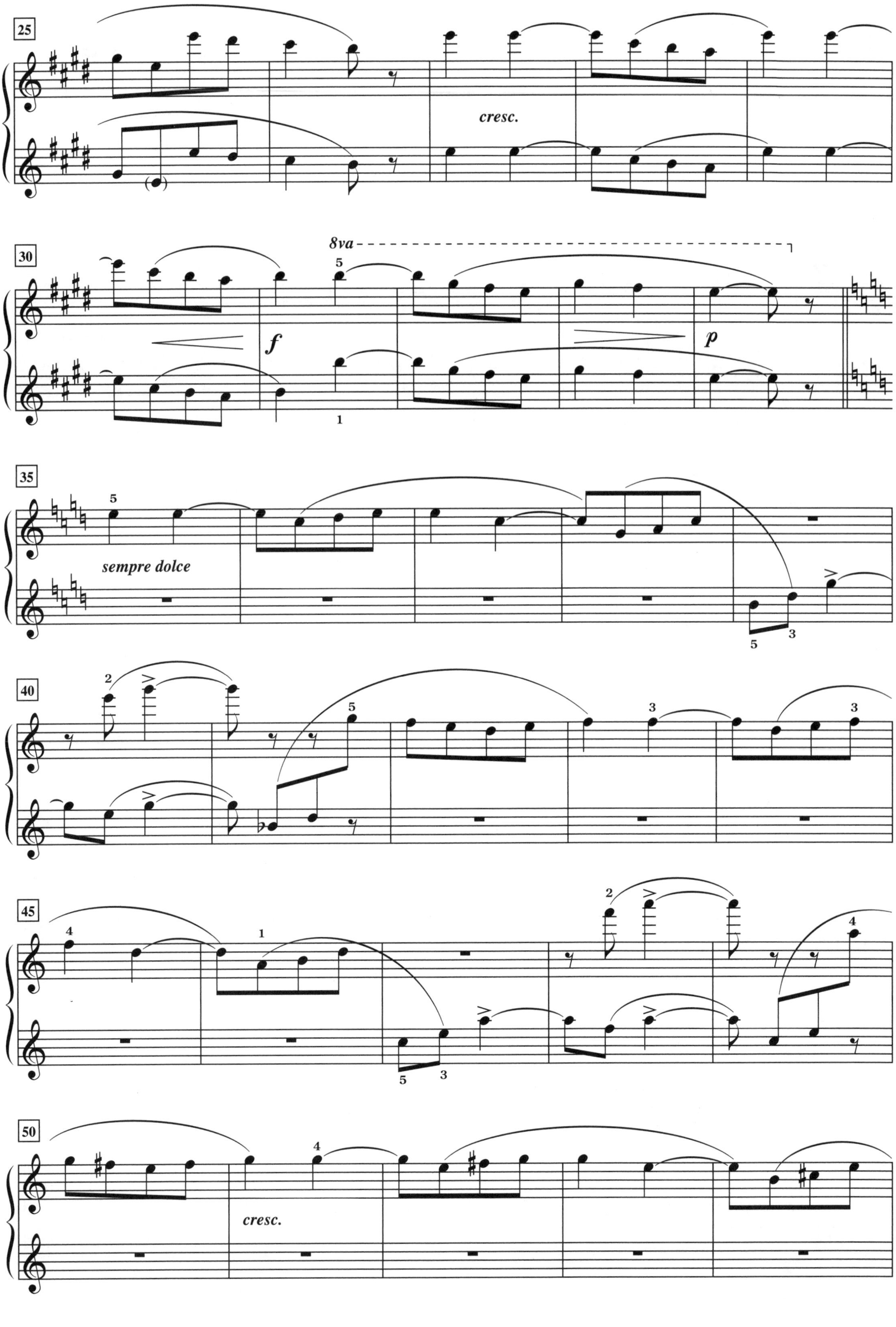

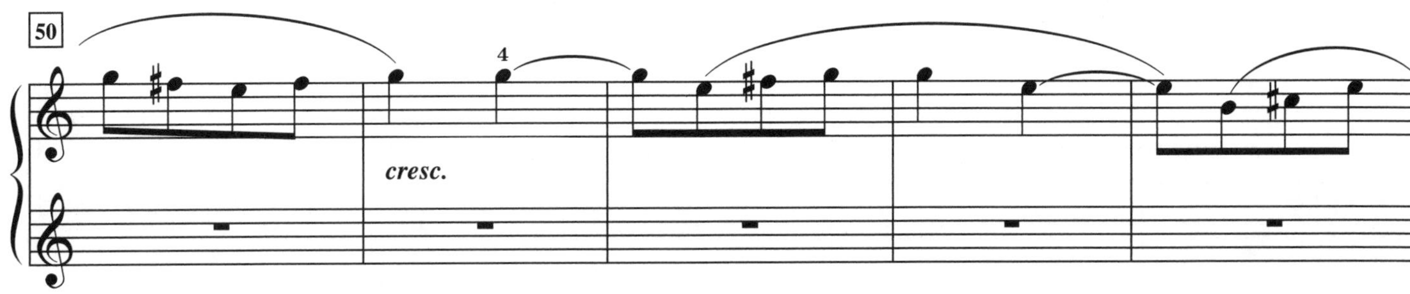

55
f
rall.
59
a tempo
p dolce
64
69
pp
74
p
79

55
8va
f
rall.
59
a tempo
pp
64
69
p
74
8va
pp
79

Waltz in E-flat Major

Secondo

Robert Fuchs (1847–1927)

Op. 25, No. 11

Langsam

p dolce *with pedal* *pp* *pp* *mf* *espressivo* *cresc.* *f* *dim.* *pp* *morendo* *rit.* *a tempo* *mf* *rit.*

Waltz in E-flat Major

PRIMO

Robert Fuchs (1847–1927)

Op. 25, No. 11

Spanish Dance

SECONDO

Moritz Moszkowski (1854–1925)
Op. 12, No. 2

Spanish Dance

PRIMO

Moritz Moszkowski (1854–1925)

Op. 12, No. 2

ⓐ Play the grace notes slightly before the beat.

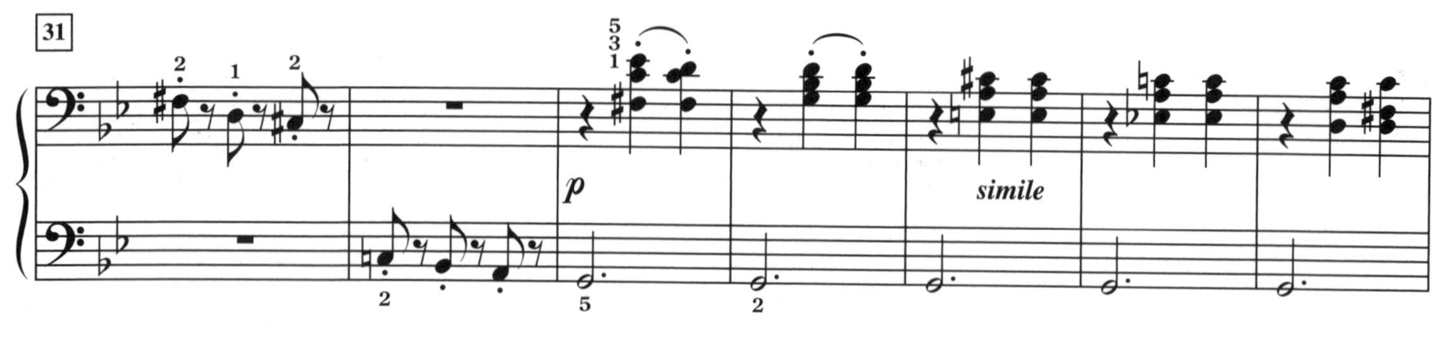
31
p
simile

38

43

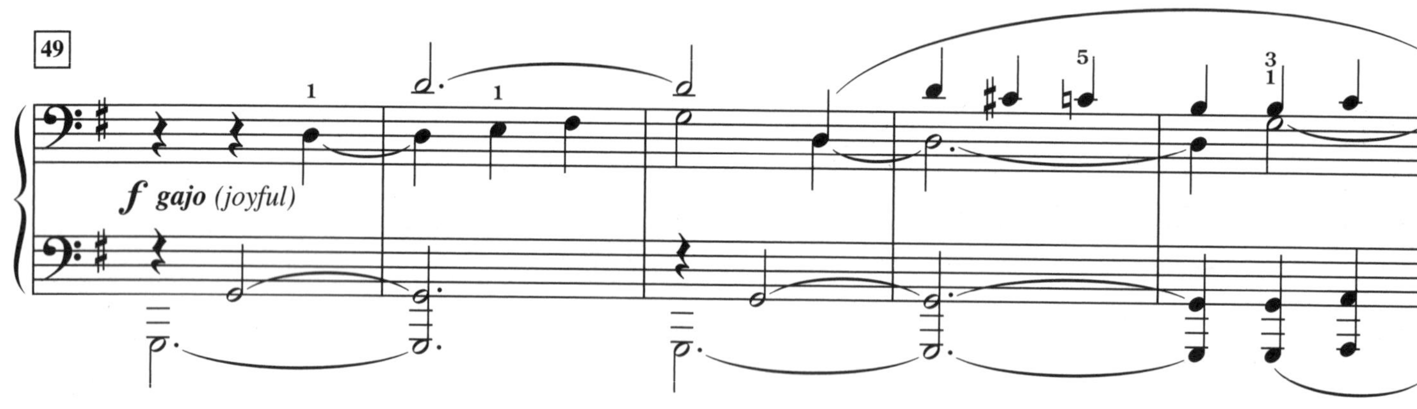
49
f gajo (joyful)

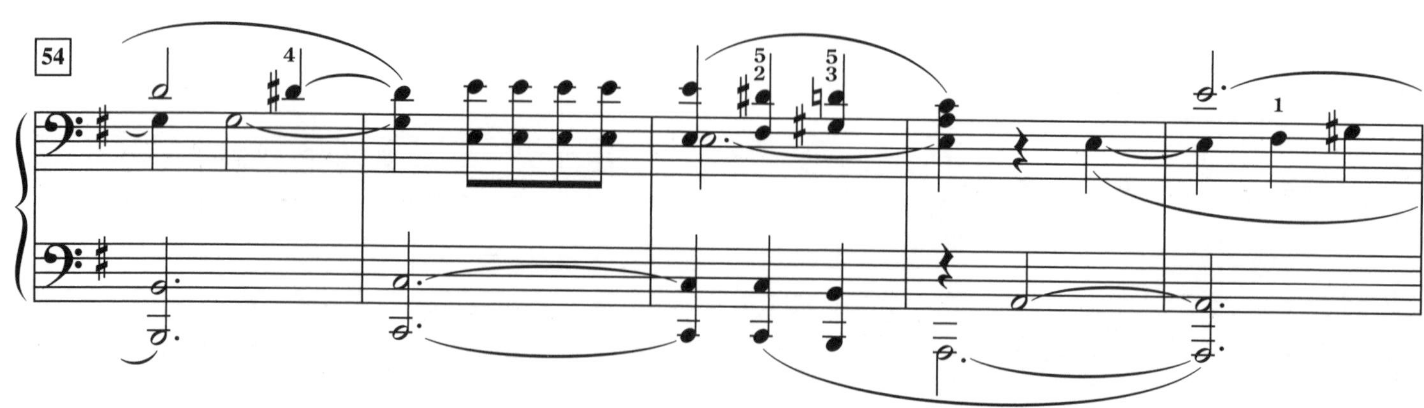
54

31
p con sentimento
38
43
f
49
gajo (joyful)
54

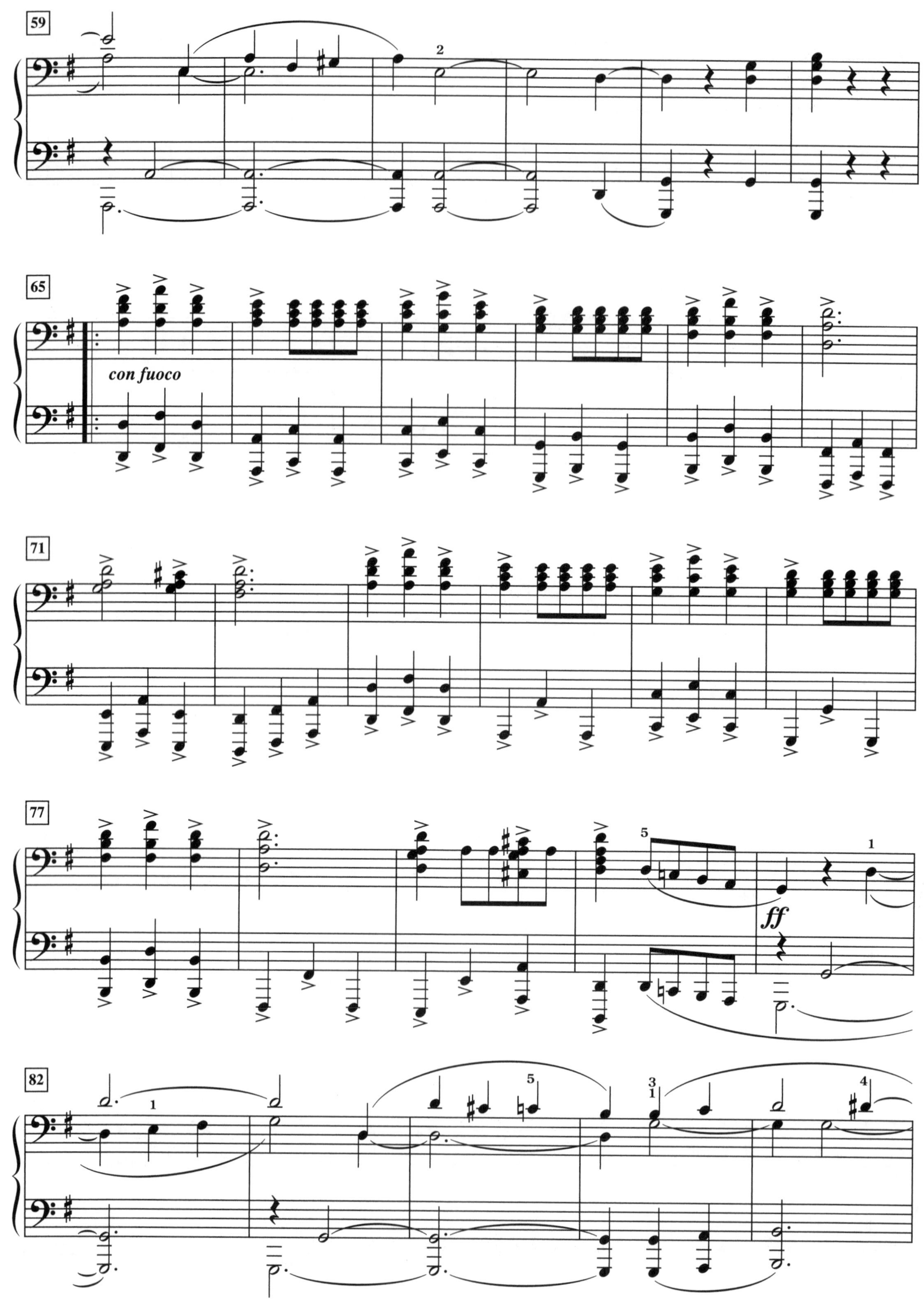
59
65
con fuoco
71
77
ff
82

59
65
con fuoco
71
sfz
77
ff
82

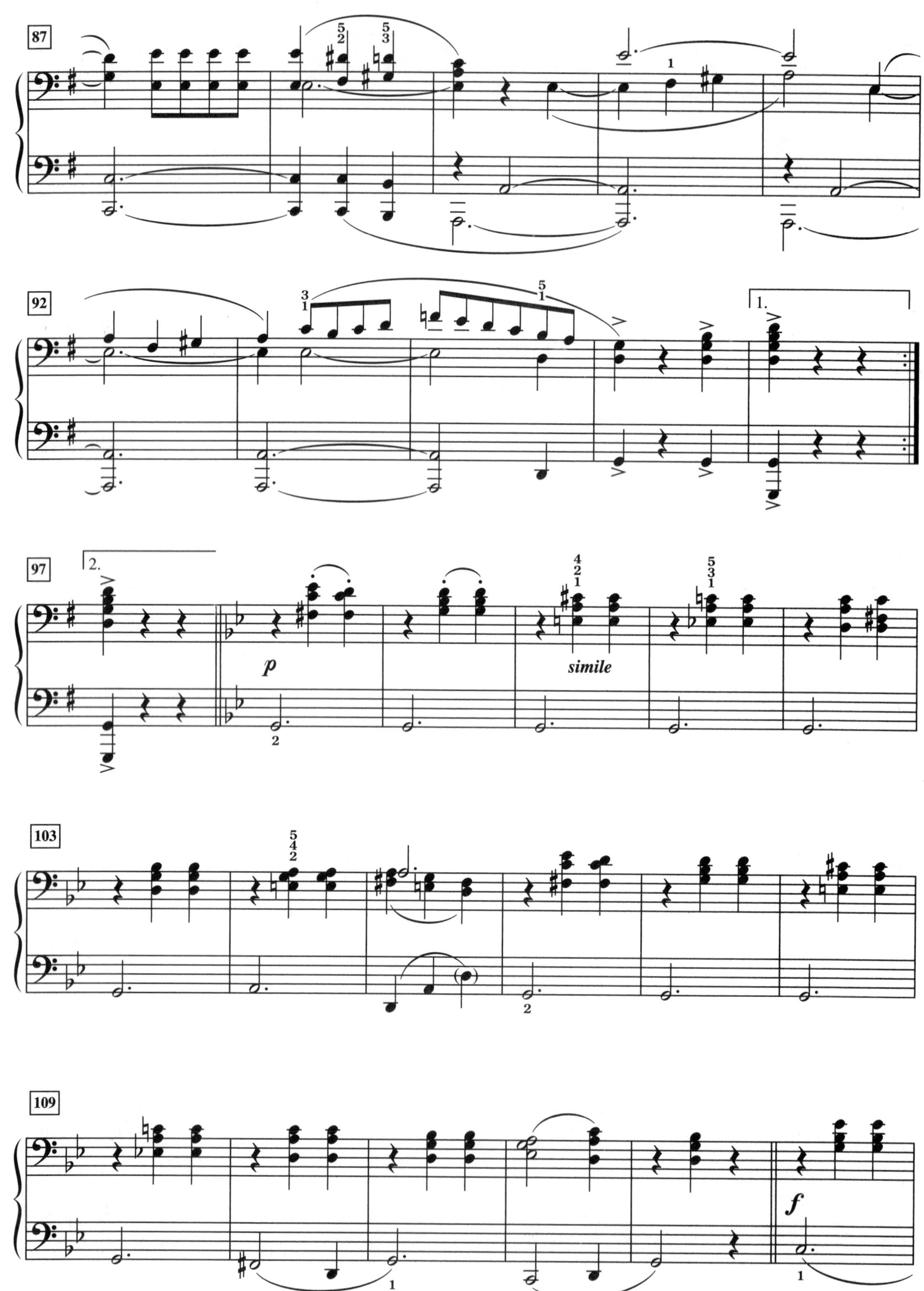
87
92
1.
97
2.
p
simile
103
109
f

87

92

1.

2.

97

p

con sentimento

103

109

f

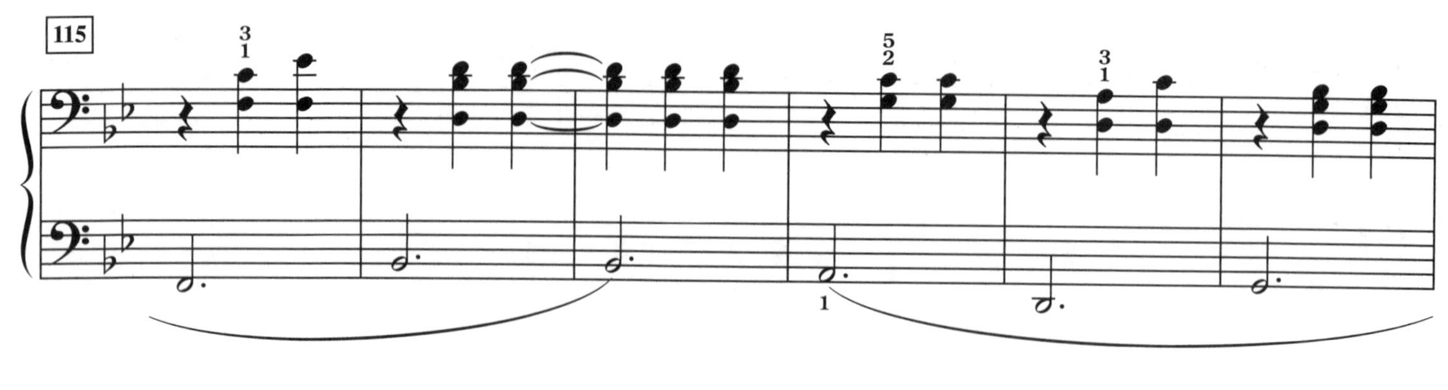
115

121
sfz
sfz
sfz

127
pp
p
simile

134

140

115
marcato un poco
121
sfz
sfz
sfz
sfz
127
p con sentimento
134
140

Trojky

from *Moravian Dances*

SECONDO

Leoš Janáček
(1854–1928)

TROJKY

from *Moravian Dances*

PRIMO

Leoš Janáček
(1854–1928)

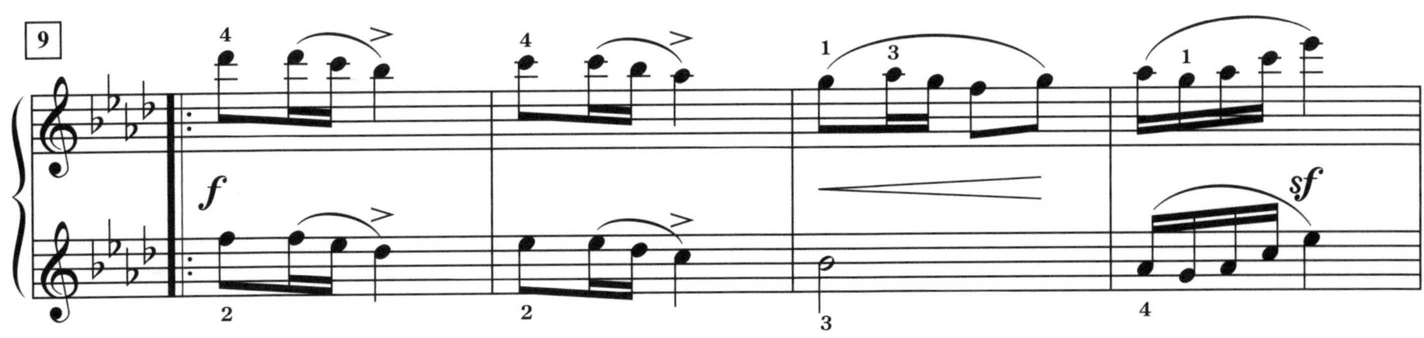

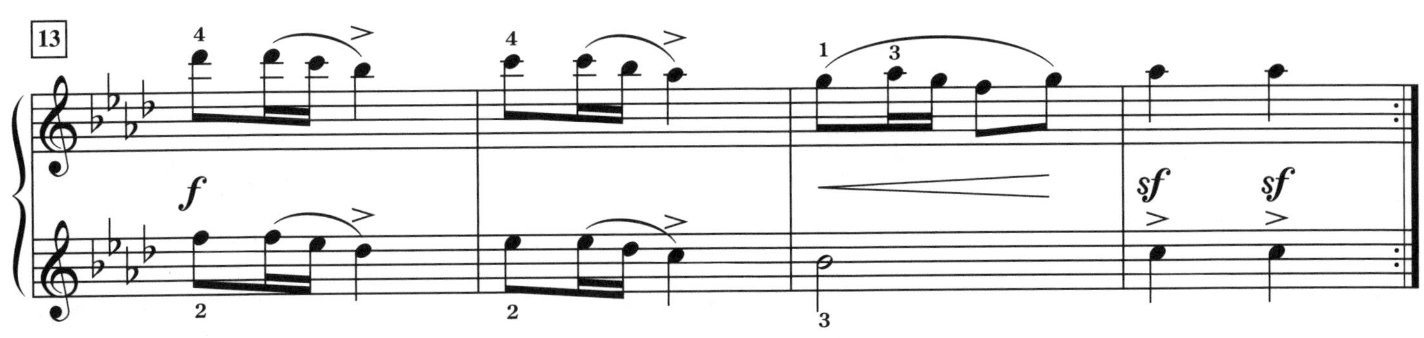

Fugue on a Russian Theme

from *6 Children's Pieces*

SECONDO

Anton Arensky (1861–1906)

Op. 34, No. 4

Fugue on a Russian Theme

from *6 Children's Pieces*

PRIMO

Anton Arensky (1861–1906)

Op. 34, No. 4

21
f
ff

25
p

29
mf
f

33
ff

37

21
25
29
33
37

41
p

45
mf
f

49
ff

53

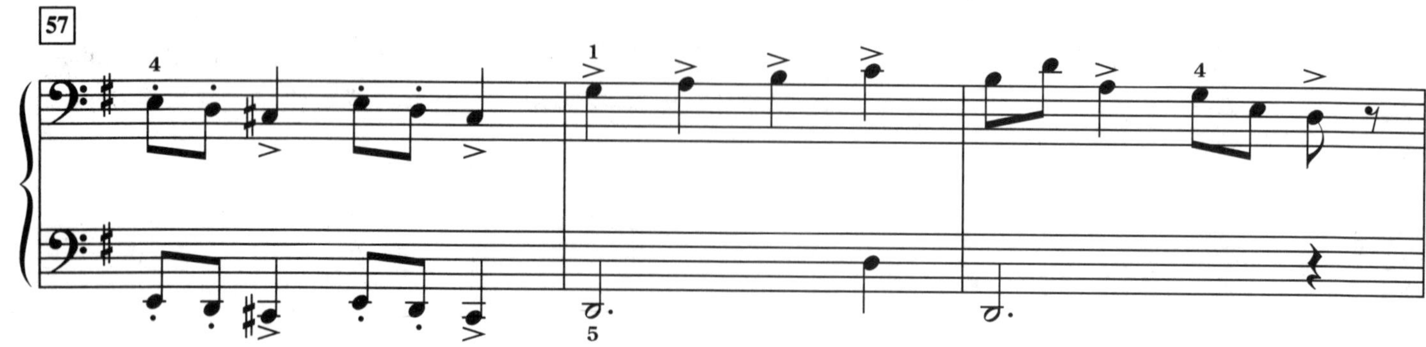
57

41
p
45
f
49
ff
53
57

60

62

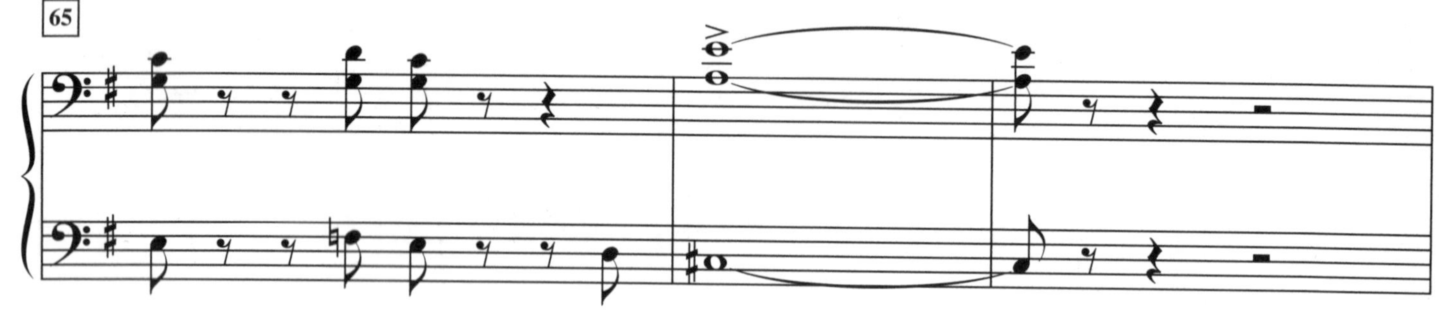
65

68
fff

71

60
62
65
68
fff
71

Menuetto

SECONDO

Anton Arensky (1861–1906)

Op. 66, No. 4

Menuetto

PRIMO

Anton Arensky (1861–1906)
Op. 66, No. 4

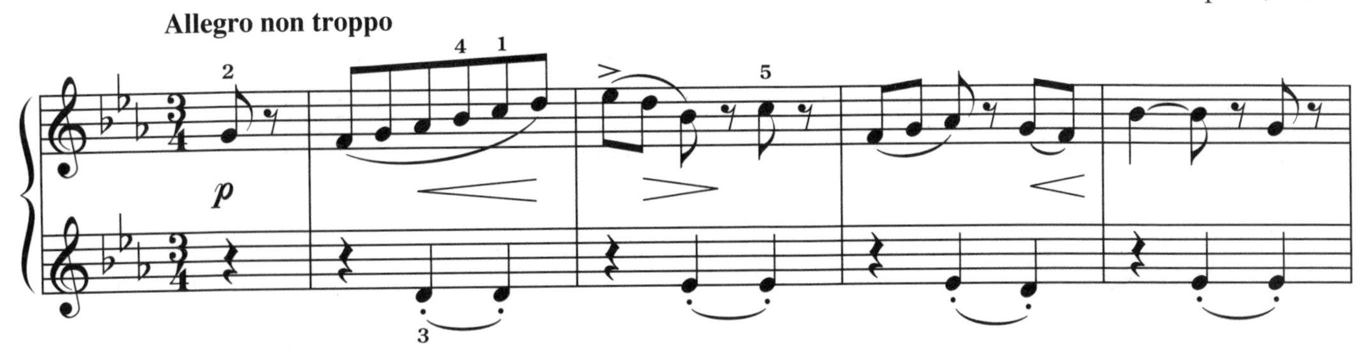

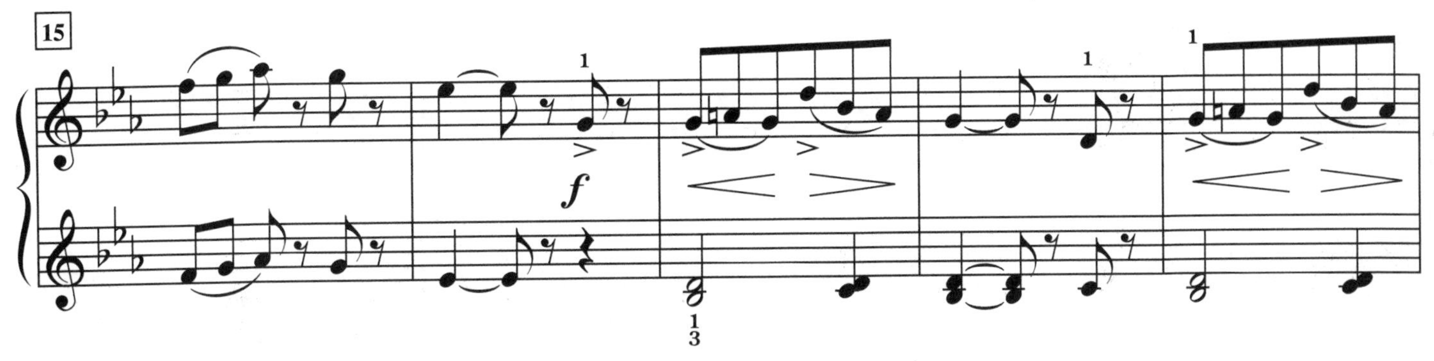

20
p

25
f

30
p

35

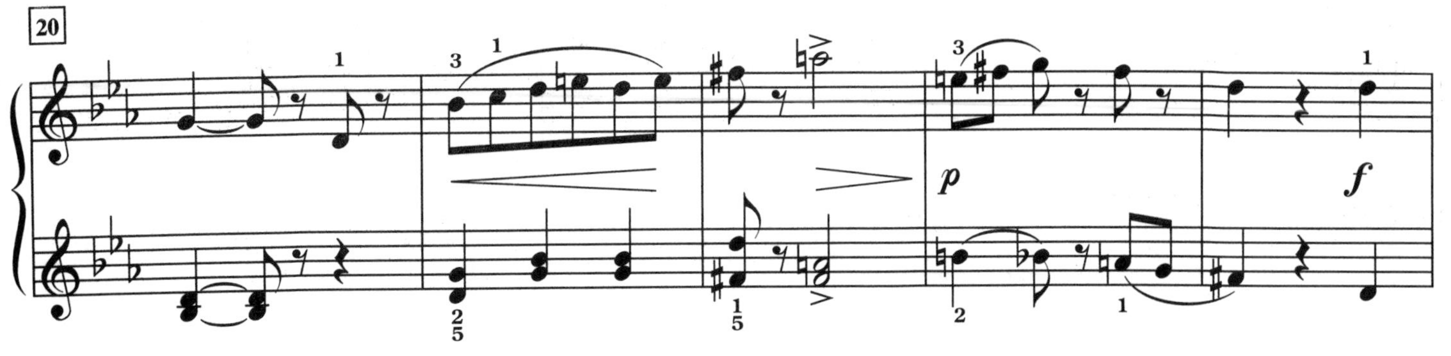

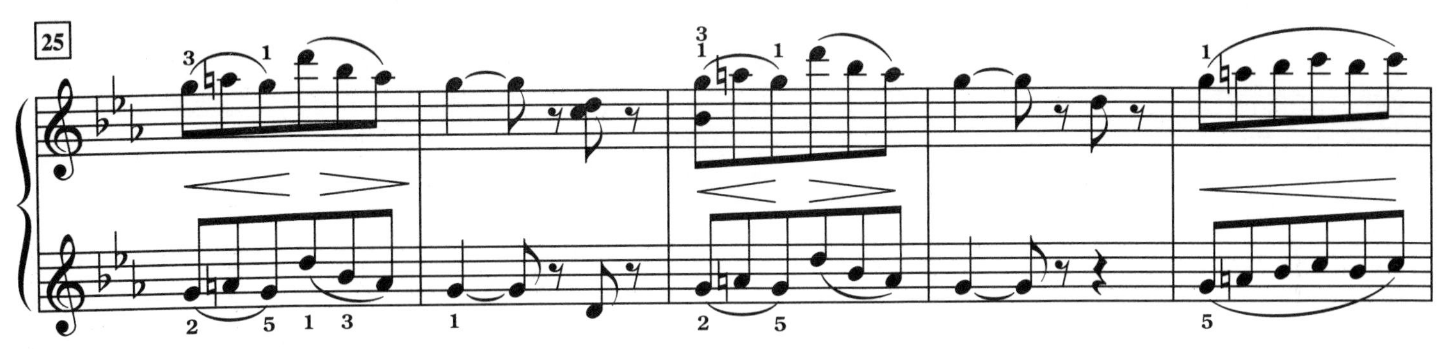

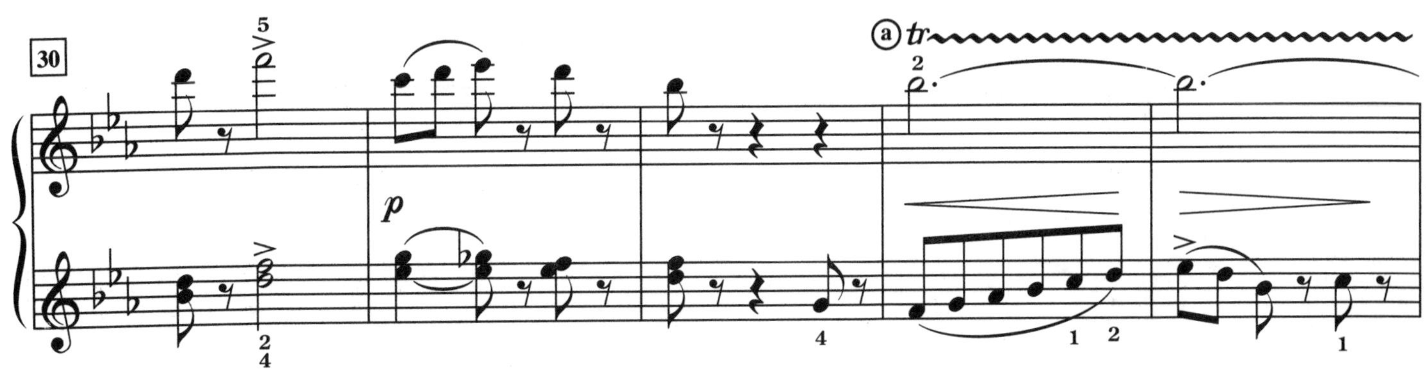

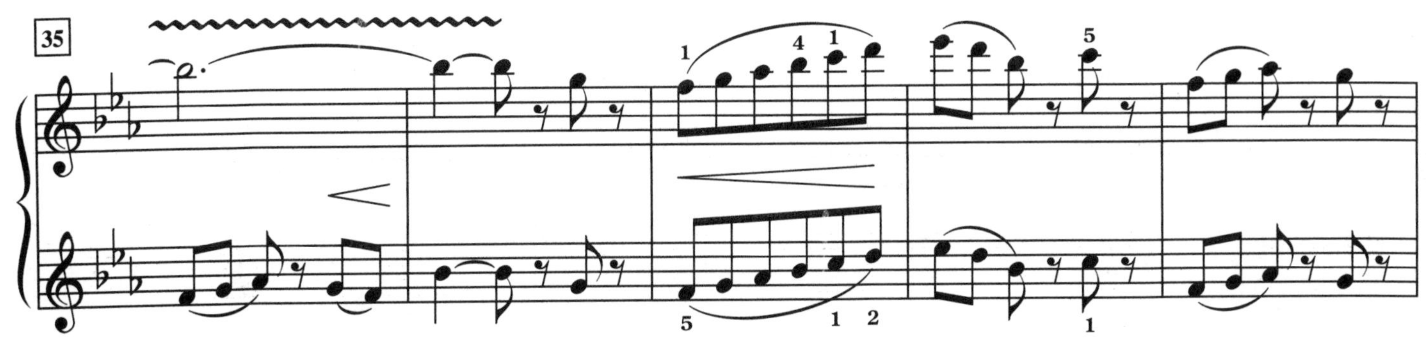

(a) Unmeasured trill beginning on B♭ and ending on B♭ on the downbeat of measure 36, beat 2.

40
f
45
p
f
50
55
p
60
poco rit.

40
f
45
p
f
50
55
p
mp
60
poco rit.

En bateau

from *Petite Suite*

SECONDO

Claude Debussy
(1862–1918)

En bateau

from *Petite Suite*

PRIMO

Claude Debussy
(1862–1918)

22
p
pp
27
31
f risoluto
f
36
p
41
p
dim.
45
p
pp

22
dim.
p
pp
27
pp
31
f risoluto
f
36
p
41
p
dim.
45
p
pp

49
pp
54
p
59
f
mf
dim.
p
65
più p
un peu retenu (a little slower)
pp
71
pp
pp
pp
77
a tempo
pp

49
pp
54
59
f
mf
dim.
p
65
un peu retenu (a little slower)
più p
pp
71
8va
pp
77
a tempo
pp

81
85
1 2 4
p
89
dim. molto
93
p
en retenant peu à peu (slowing little by little)
97
più p
dim.
pp
104
encore plus retenu (still slower)
pp

PRIMO

81

85

p

pp

89

dim. molto

93

p

97

en retenant peu à peu *(slowing little by little)*

più p

dim.

pp

encore plus retenu *(still slower)*

Andalusierin

SECONDO

Ede (Eduard) Poldini
(1869–1957)

Andalusierin

PRIMO

Ede (Eduard) Poldini
(1869–1957)

ⓐ Play the grace notes slightly before the beat.

31

37

43

pp

49

Più vivo

pp

55

61

31
37
cresc.
dim.
43
p
49
Più vivo
8va
pp
55
61
cresc.

67
pp
73
79
85
sf
91
p
Tempo I
pp
97

67
dim.
pp
73
79
8va
cresc.
dim.
85
f
91
Tempo I
p
97

SECONDO

103

109

115

121

127

134 Vivo

p *pp* *dim.*

103
109
cresc.
115
dim.
p
121
p
127
dim.
pp
134
Vivo
8va
pp
pp

LE JARDIN FÉERIQUE

from *Ma mère l'oye*

SECONDO

Maurice Ravel
(1875–1937)

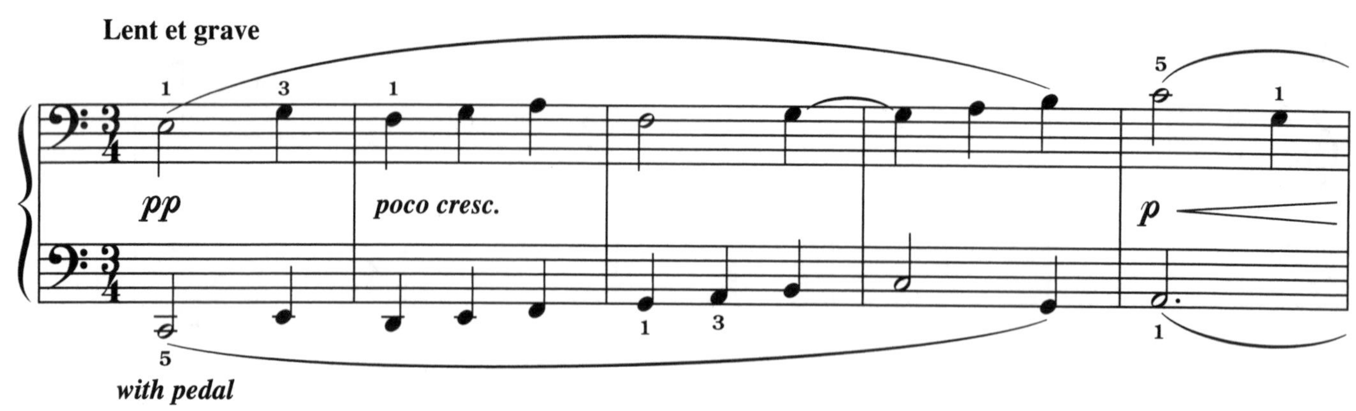

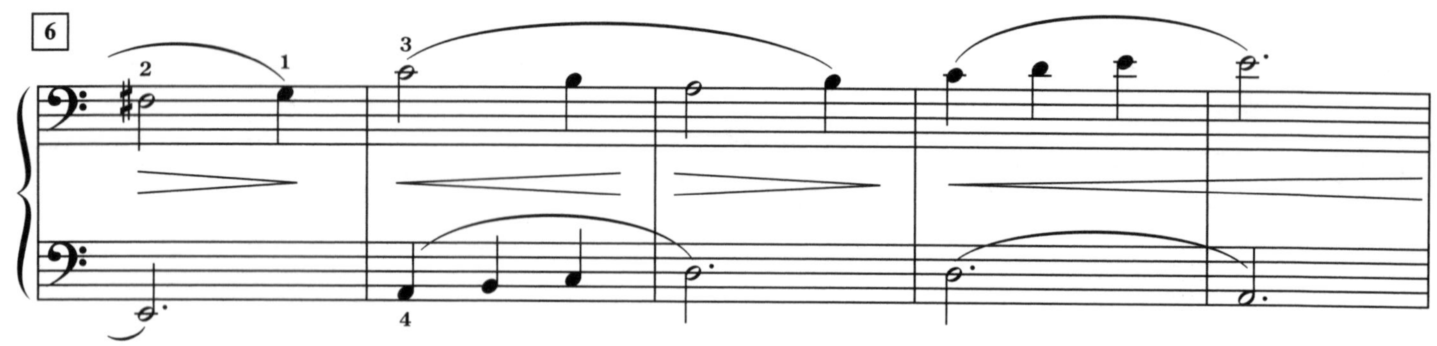

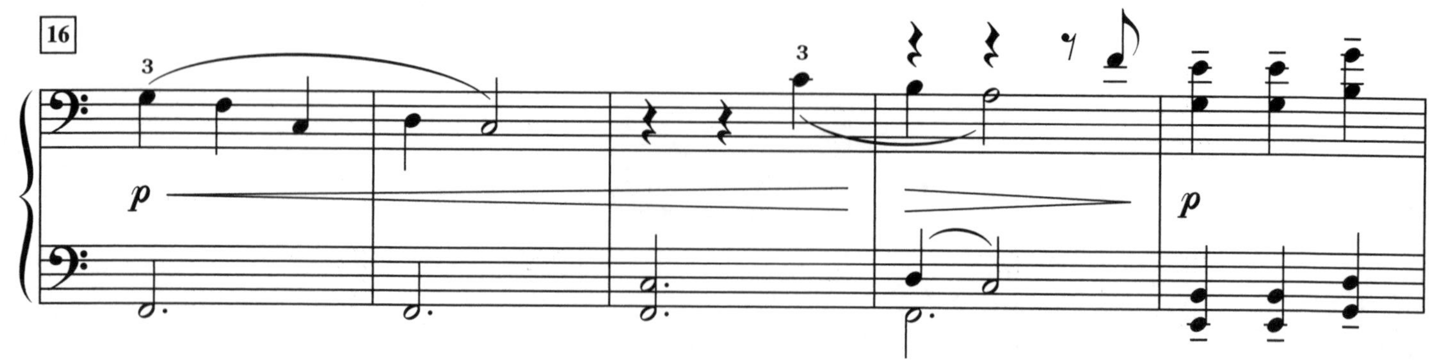

Le jardin féerique

from *Ma mère l'oye*

PRIMO

Maurice Ravel
(1875–1937)

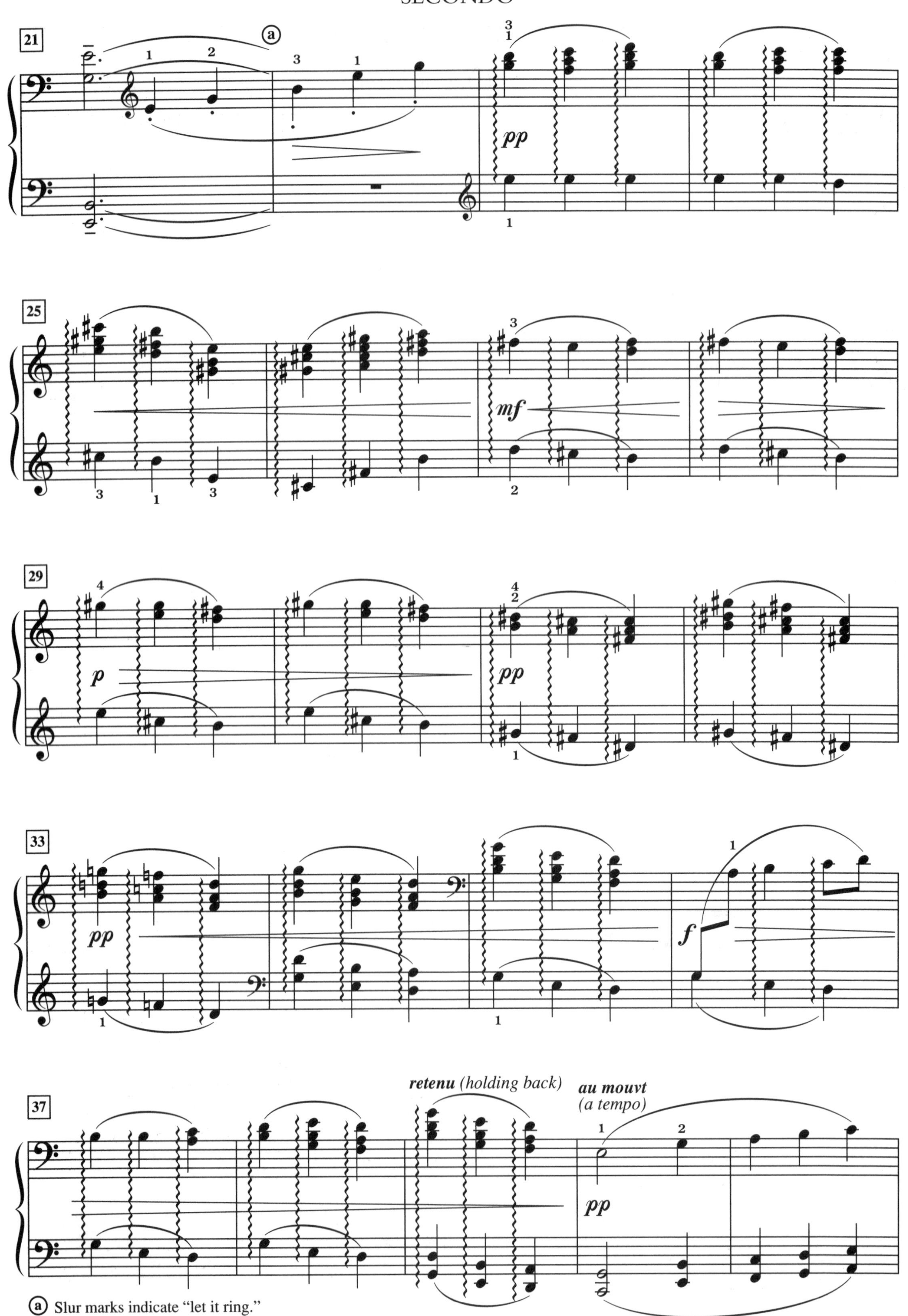

ⓐ Slur marks indicate "let it ring."

ⓐ Slur marks indicate "let it ring."

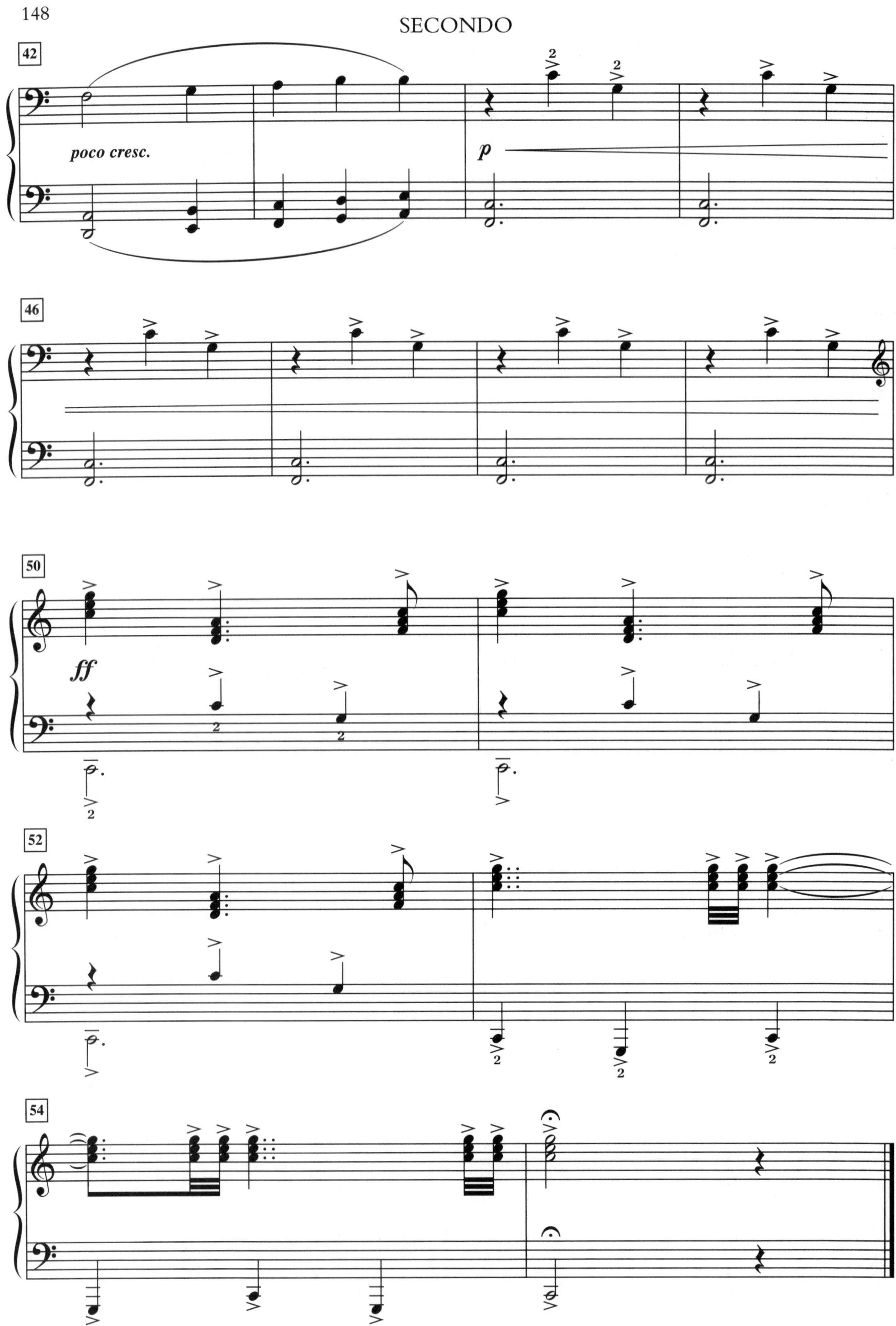
42
poco cresc.
p
46
50
ff
52
54

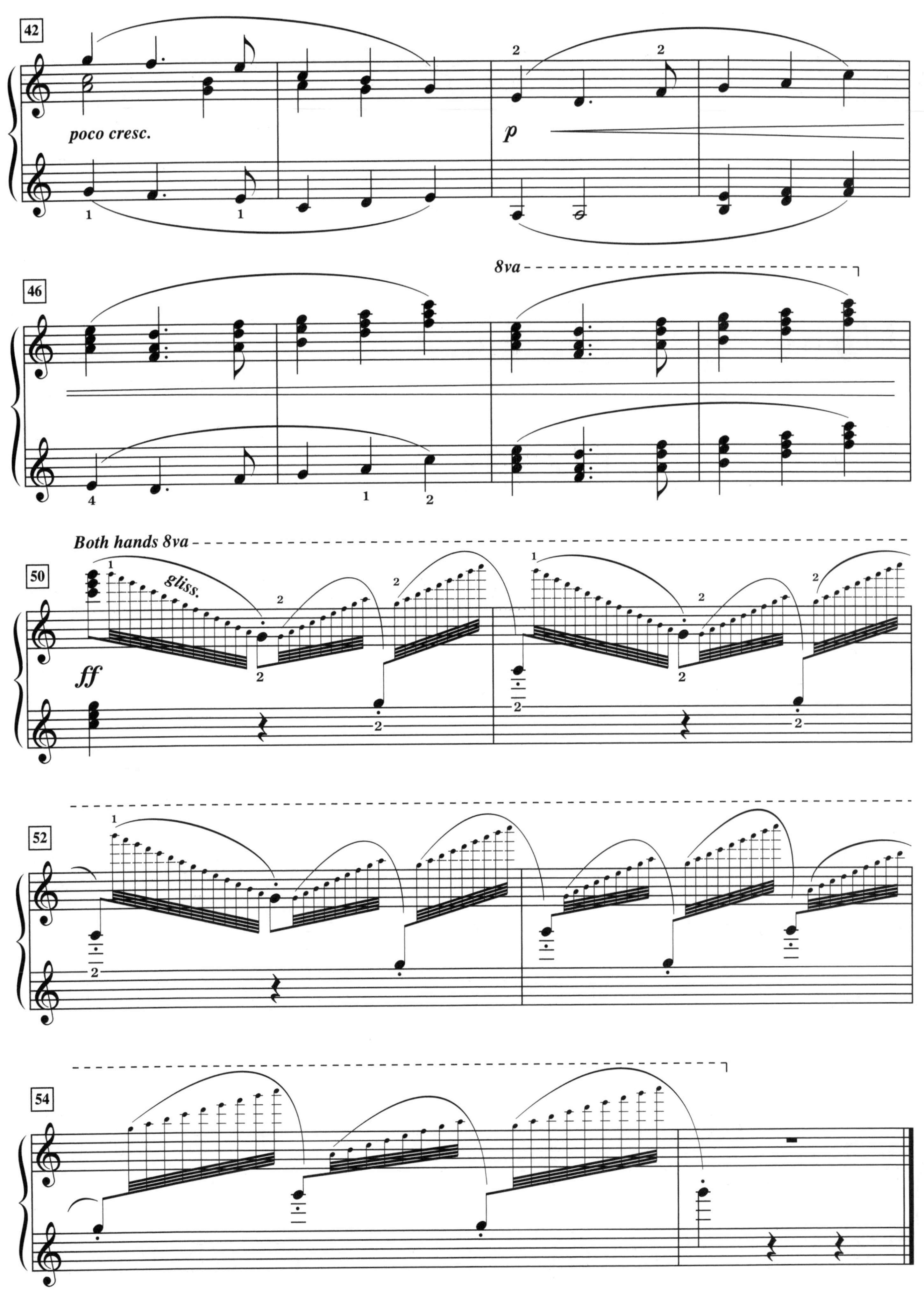
42
poco cresc.
p
46
8va
Both hands 8va
50
gliss.
ff
52
54

Russian Dance

SECONDO

Serge Bortkiewicz (1877–1952)
Op. 18, No. 2

Russian Dance

PRIMO

Serge Bortkiewicz (1877–1952)

Op. 18, No. 2

(a) Play the grace notes slightly before the beat.

Più allegro
pp
1.
2.
mf
rit.

Più allegro
8va
pp
mf
rit.

61
riten. poco a poco
67
Allegro
mf
72
riten. poco a poco
78
dim.
84
Andantino (Tempo I)
pp

61

2.

riten. poco a poco

67

Allegro

mf

72

riten. poco a poco

78

dim.

84

Andantino (Tempo I)

p

dolce

90
p
96
p
102
rit.
109
Sostenuto
pp dolce
u.c.
114
Lento
pp
ppp

90
8va
p
96
p
102
rit.
109
Sostenuto
pp
114
Lento
pp
ppp

About the Composers

Anton André (1775–1842) was a German pianist, violinist, composer and publisher. His book on harmony and counterpoint was highly respected during his lifetime. Mozart created a catalog of his own works that André published in 1841.

Anton Arensky (1861–1906) was a Russian pianist, composer and conductor. Among his theory students at the Moscow Conservatory were Rachmaninoff and Scriabin. Although Arensky studied composition with Rimsky-Korsakov, his music is known for its lyrical melodies influenced by Chopin and Tchaikovsky.

Ernesto Becucci (1845–1905), an Italian composer and teacher, is best known for the light style and character of his piano works. He also wrote sacred music, songs and several sets of piano duets.

Ludwig van Beethoven (1770–1827), the famous German composer, is known throughout the world for his creative genius. His symphonies, concertos, chamber music and piano sonatas are recognized as his greatest masterpieces. Beginning in 1802, he experienced hearing loss and was completely deaf before the end of his life; however, he continued his energetic compositional process without interruption.

Georges Bizet (1838–1875) was a French composer who is known primarily for his operas—his best-known is *Carmen*—but he also wrote over 150 works for piano. He studied both composition and piano at the Paris Conservatory and developed into a brilliant pianist.

Serge Bortkiewicz (1877–1952) was a Russian pianist and composer who spent much of his adult life in Berlin and Vienna. After studying at the St. Petersburg and Leipzig Conservatories, he played concerts throughout Germany, Australia, Hungary, France and Russia, often featuring his own works. His compositional style was influenced by Liszt, Chopin and Tchaikovsky.

Johannes Brahms (1833–1897) is one of the most famous German composers of the Romantic period. His orchestral, choral, piano, vocal and chamber works are performed frequently on concerts throughout the world. The duet by Brahms in this collection is from the *Waltzes,* Op. 39, written in 1865.

Carl Czerny (1791–1857) was an Austrian pianist, teacher and composer. He taught only talented students and devoted the remainder of his time to composition and arranging. He published almost 1,000 compositions during his lifetime, with numerous manuscripts left unpublished.

Claude Debussy (1862–1918), a French composer, is considered the creator of musical Impressionism. At the age of 10, he entered the Paris Conservatory where he studied piano, solfege and harmony. He greatly influenced 20th-century music through his use of modes, whole-tone and pentatonic scales, tonal ambiguity, unresolved chords, and parallel intervals (especially 4ths and 5ths).

Anton Diabelli (1781–1858), an Austrian publisher and composer, wrote numerous piano duets. He was the publisher of Schubert's first printed works. A versatile musician, piano teacher and composer, he was able to respond to musical trends of the day. Consequently, his publishing company was a huge financial success.

Jan Ladislav Dussek (1760–1812), born in Bohemia, was a composer and keyboard virtuoso. A student of C. P. E. Bach for a brief time, he taught and performed throughout Europe. He was among the first composers to use virtuosic writing in his piano music—a practice followed by many 19th-century composers. He and Clementi are credited with introducing the "singing touch" in piano performance.

Gabriel Fauré (1845–1924), a French composer whose musical style foreshadowed Impressionism, was a professor of composition at the Paris Conservatory. While he was never a popular composer during his lifetime, music connoisseurs were nonetheless attracted to his songs, piano pieces and chamber music. He rejected virtuosity in his piano music, and his songs are known for their melodic lines. He taught many famous musicians including Maurice Ravel.

Robert Fuchs (1847–1927) was an Austrian composer and teacher. He studied at the Vienna Conservatory and later taught there as a professor of harmony. Among his students were Gustav Mahler, Jean Sibelius and Hugo Wolf. Johannes Brahms, a friend of Fuchs, greatly admired his work.

Niels Wilhelm Gade (1817–1890), a Danish composer, was a founder of the Copenhagen Conservatory where he taught composition and music history. A friend of Felix Mendelssohn, his music shows influences from both Mendelssohn and Robert Schumann. Although he wrote primarily in a Romantic style, he used Danish folk melodies in his music and led the way for further development of Scandinavian music.

Leoš Janáček (1854–1928) was a Czech composer, known for his operas. He taught composition at the Prague Conservatory, and much of his music was performed in that city. Many themes from folk songs that he collected in Moravia can be found in his music. His musical style was also influenced by Mussorgsky and the French Impressionists.

Friedrich Kuhlau (1786–1832) was a German composer and pianist. After 1810, he lived in Copenhagen where he gained recognition as a teacher and concert pianist. During a visit to Vienna, he met Beethoven, a composer whose works were often included on his concert programs. As a composer, he is best known for his piano music—especially his sonatinas, which are popular teaching pieces.

Ignaz Moscheles (1794–1870), a German, was a virtuoso pianist, teacher and composer. He studied in Prague and Vienna, where he knew Beethoven. His piano students at the Leipzig Conservatory came from all over the world. Among them was Mendelssohn, who became his close friend.

Moritz Moszkowski (1854–1925) was a German pianist, teacher and composer. He toured as a concert pianist throughout Germany, England and in Paris, but his performing career was interrupted by an arm injury. In 1897, he settled in Paris. His *Spanish Dances,* Op. 12, for one piano, four hands, were so popular that he later arranged them for solo piano.

Ede (Eduard) Poldini (1869–1957) was a Hungarian composer who studied at the Budapest National Conservatory as well as in Vienna. His compositions were influenced by contemporary German and French trends, with Hungarian folk elements added. He wrote choral music and songs, as well as works for the stage and for piano.

Maurice Ravel (1875–1937), a famous French composer, was a student of Fauré at the Paris Conservatory. He composed music for stage, orchestra, chamber groups, voice and piano. Although he was never on the faculty of any school, Ravel is one of the best known of the French Impressionist composers.

Carl Reinecke (1824–1910) was a German pianist, composer, conductor and teacher. He taught piano and composition at both the Cologne and Leipzig Conservatories. His yearly concert tours throughout Europe often featured the music of Mozart. He is especially recognized for his music written for children.

Franz Schubert (1797–1828), a major Austrian composer of the Romantic period, was known as the creator of vocal lieder, songs that convey deep emotions through both the music and the words. Schubert wrote numerous vocal works, as well as works for all instruments. He wrote many piano duets that appear frequently on concert programs throughout the world.

Robert Schumann (1810–1856) was a German composer whose music expresses the spirit of the Romantic period. After a brief period in law school, Schumann studied piano with Friedrich Wieck and later married Wieck's daughter Clara, a famous concert pianist from her childhood. Throughout his life, he was plagued by psychological problems; nevertheless, he was recognized as one of the most significant composers from that era. His most important works are for piano, voice, orchestra, and chamber ensembles.

Robert Volkmann (1815–1883) was a German composer who was encouraged by Robert Schumann. He spent most of his adult life in Budapest, where he taught at the National Academy of Music. Volkmann composed in almost all genres, but some of his most successful works were character pieces for piano, written for children.